F.A.I.T.H. Confessions

Regina A. Price

So then faith comes by hearing, and hearing by the word of God.
Romans 10:17

F.A.I.T.H. Confessions
Copyright © 2017 by Regina Price
All rights reserved.

F.A.I.T.H. Confessions

Printed in the United States of America.

ISBN: 978069292482-2

Book Designed by: SmallBizNiz.com

Editing by: Pastors Sean and Kim Walsh

For information visit: www.alite4life.com

F.A.I.T.H. Confessions

Your walk with God is contingent upon your faith in God. No man has seen God at any time, ("you cannot see my face, for no one may see me and live" Exodus 33:20) yet we believe and confess through faith that He is God, He exists and He rewards those who diligently seek Him.

The late Smith Wigglesworth, God's Apostle of Faith, performed many healing miracles based upon the principles of God's word and his F.A.I.T.H. Confessions. His ministry is summed up in his own words: "First, read the Word of God. Second, consume the Word of God until it consumes you. Third, believe the Word of God. Fourth, act on the word". "So then faith comes by hearing, and hearing by the word of God" (Romans 10:17). "Also faith by itself, if it does not have works, is dead!" (James 2:7) This means you must "Ignite your faith!" God told Habakkuk to write the vision and make it plain so that others who read it may understand it with ease. It was very important that Habakkuk put his faith in action by legibly writing out the vision that God revealed to him, for the vision is yet for an appointed time (Habakkuk 2:2-3 Paraphrased). When you make F.A.I.T.H. Confessions, know that God will manifest them at His appointed time.

What Is Faith?

Faith is confidence in the word of God. Now faith is the substance of things hoped for that you do not see with the physical eye but believe that it's there. Faith is saying it before you see it! When you call those things that are not as though they were and make F.A.I.T.H. Confessions, you apply the spiritual principle of God's Word that He is obligated to fulfill. "The word of the Lord came to me: "What do you see, Jeremiah?" "I see the branch of an almond tree" I replied. Then said the

F.A.I.T.H. Confessions

Lord to me, "You have seen correctly: for I am watching to see that my word is fulfilled." (Jeremiah 1:11-12)

"By faith Abel offered unto God a more excellent sacrifice than Cain, by which he obtained witness that he was righteous, God testifying of his gifts: and by it he being dead yet speaks. By faith Enoch was transformed that he should not see death; and was not found, because God had taken him: in other words, Enoch did not experience a physical death. Before his transformation he had this testimony, that he pleased God.

By faith Noah, being warned of God of things not seen as yet, moved with fear, prepared an ark to the saving of his house; by that which he condemned the world, and became heir of the righteousness which is by faith. By faith Abraham, when he was called to go out into a place which he should after receive for an inheritance, obeyed; and he went out, not knowing where he went. Through faith also Sarah herself received strength to conceive seed, and was delivered of a child when she was past age, because she judged him faithful who had promised" (Hebrews 11:4-11).

Faith is not based on what you see but what God said. Make these F.A.I.T.H. Confessions on a daily basis as you spend your time with the Lord and I decree and declare everything you have spoken through faith according to the word of God shall manifest itself in your life at God's appointed time.

So then faith comes by hearing,
And hearing by the word of God.
Romans 10:17

Father, I thank you that my ears are attentive
To hear the word of God;
Your word is truth.

F.A.I.T.H. Confessions

Now faith is the substance of things hoped for,
The evidence of things not seen.
Hebrews 11:1

Father, I thank you that I don't have to
See it to believe it,
I believe that all the things I have hoped for
Will show up at the appointed time.

For we walk by faith, not by sight.
2 Corinthians 5:7

🐟

Father, I thank you that my faith is in you
Not what I can see
If I can see it, it is temporary and
Subject to change.

F.A.I.T.H. Confessions

Then Jesus said to him,
"Go your way; your faith has made you well."
And immediately he received his sight
And followed Jesus on the road
Mark 10:52

Father, I thank you that my faith makes me well.
Therefore, I speak total healing over my
Spirit, Soul and Body
According to your word and my faith.

Therefore I say to you, whatever things
You ask when you pray,
Believe that you receive them,
And you will have them.
Mark 11:24

Father, I thank you that when I mix
My faith with my prayers,
You hear me and I will receive
Whatever I ask you in prayer.

F.A.I.T.H. Confessions

For in it the righteousness of God is
Revealed from faith to faith;
As it is written, "The just shall live by faith."
Romans 1:17

Father God, I thank you that I am a
Respectable and honest person.
I walk by faith in Christ Jesus,
And not in any good deeds of my own.
I thank you that as I meditate on your word
My faith will be strengthened.

Fight the good fight of faith,
Lay hold on eternal life,
To which you were also called,
When you made your good confession
In the presence of many witnesses.
1 Timothy 6:12

Father, I thank you that my faith will not fail me.
I will continue to fight the good fight of faith
And I will see the goodness of the Lord.

F.A.I.T.H. Confessions

If you declare with your mouth, "Jesus is Lord,"
And believe in your heart that
God raised him from the dead,
You will be saved.
For it is with your heart that
You believe and are justified,
And it is with your mouth that you
Profess your faith and are saved.
Romans 10:9-10 NIV

Father God, I thank you that
I confess with my mouth,
And believe in my heart,
That Jesus is Lord.
And I will live for Him in the earth as
He shows me how
And I will live with Him in eternity!

So Jesus said to them, "Because of your unbelief;
For assuredly, I say to you,
If you have faith as a mustard seed,
You will say to this mountain,
'Move from here to there,'
And it will move; and nothing will
Be impossible for you.
Matthew 17:20

Father, I thank you that my faith is
Rooted and planted like a small mustard seed,
And I thank you that when it grows,
I have more than enough
Faith to believe anything is possible.

F.A.I.T.H. Confessions

Now may the God of hope fill you with
All joy and peace in believing,
That you may abound in hope by the
Power of the Holy Spirit.
Romans 15:13

Father God, I thank you for hope,
Joy and peace in my life.
You have filled me with your strength and power
And I can face any obstacle through faith
Because Holy Spirit lives inside of me.

For God so loved the world that
He gave His only begotten Son,
That whoever believes in Him should not
Perish but have everlasting life.
John 3:16

Father, I thank you for giving me eternal life
Through your Son Jesus and on
The confession of my faith,
I commit to giving to others just
As you have done for me.

But let him ask in faith, with no doubting,
For he who doubts is like a wave of the sea
Driven and tossed by the wind.
James 1:6

Father, I thank you that your word is truth
And I do not doubt it in my heart;
I believe it will accomplish everything
That it was sent in my life to do.

REGINA PRICE

Be on your guard; stand firm in the faith;
Be courageous; be strong.
1 Corinthians 16:13

Father, I thank you that I fear
No man but stand strong
In my faith knowing that you
Will never leave me or forsake me;
You will be with me until the end of the world.

F.A.I.T.H. Confessions

For it is by grace you have been saved
Through faith and this is not from yourselves
It is the gift of God not by works
So that no one can boast.
Ephesians 2:8-9

Father, I thank you that your
Grace and your mercy is sufficient for me.
Therefore, I am not destroyed
Your mercies are new every morning;
Great is your faithfulness.

Then Jesus told him,
"Because you have seen me, you have believed;
Blessed are those who have
Not seen and yet have believed."
John 20:29

Father, I thank you for your precious Holy Spirit.
He bears witness that you are my God
And I am your child, therefore,
I have faith and I believe.

F.A.I.T.H. Confessions

For this very reason, make every effort
To add to your faith goodness;
And to goodness, knowledge;
And to knowledge, self-control;
And to self-control, perseverance;
And to perseverance, godliness;
And to godliness, mutual affection;
And to mutual affection, love.
2 Peter 1:5-7

Father, I acknowledge that these ingredients
Are important to strengthen my faith
But the greatest of these is "Love".

The Lord had said to Abram,
"Go from your country,
Your people and your father's household
To the land I will show you.
Genesis 12:1

Father, I thank you that Abraham
Had faith and believed you.
Therefore, I too have faith
To go where you say go
And do what you say do, Amen!

F.A.I.T.H. Confessions

Your servant has killed both lion and bear;
And this uncircumcised Philistine
Will be like one of them,
Seeing he has defied the armies of the living God.
1 Samuel 17:36

Father, I thank you that I do not have the spirit
Of fear, but faith, and I am more than
Able to conquer the lion, the bear and the giants
That come up against me. I am victorious!

And by faith even Sarah,
Who was past childbearing age
Was enabled to bear children
Because she considered him faithful
Who had made the promise.
Hebrews 11:11

Father, I thank you that there is
Nothing too hard for you!
You kept your promise to give
Sarah a child at an old age
And you will keep your promises to me.
Your promises are yes and Amen.

F.A.I.T.H. Confessions

And now these three remain: Faith, hope and love.
But the greatest of these is love.
1 Corinthians 13:13

Father, I confess that God is love; therefore,
I choose to love my neighbor as myself.
If I do not love my neighbor who I see everyday
How can I have faith to love God?

For whatever is born of God
Is victorious over the world;
And this is the victory that conquers the world,
Even our faith.
1 John 5:4

Because I have been born of God,
I am victorious in the earth.
God is so good and He is so great
And my faith conquers everything.

F.A.I.T.H. Confessions

Looking unto Jesus the author and
Finisher of our faith;
Who for the joy that was set before him
Endured the cross, despising the shame,
And is set down at the right
Hand of the throne of God.
Hebrews 12:2

Father, thank you that your
Undying love for me makes
My joy complete and your word
Makes my faith strong, therefore,
I have an expected end.

REGINA PRICE

No weapon formed against you shall prosper,
And every tongue which rises
Against you in judgment
You shall condemn.
This is the heritage of the servants
Of the Lord, And their righteousness is
From Me, Says the Lord.
Isaiah 54:17

Father, I thank you that when my enemies
Come upon me like a flood, your spirit in me will
Lift up a standard against them
And they shall not overtake me.

F.A.I.T.H. Confessions

Thus also faith by itself,
If it does not have works, is dead.
James 2:17

Father, I thank you that with
The help of Holy Spirit
I will put my faith and my works in action
To carry out your assignments for me in the earth.

And suddenly, a woman who had a flow of blood
For twelve years came from behind
And touched the hem of His garment.
For she said to herself,
"If only I may touch His garment,
I shall be made well.
Matthew 9:20-21

Father, I thank you that life and death are
In my tongue; therefore, I speak life.
I shall live and not die
To fulfill God's purpose for me in the earth.

F.A.I.T.H. Confessions

Above all, taking the shield of faith,
Wherewith ye shall be able to quench
All the fiery darts of the wicked.
Ephesians 6:16

Father, I thank you that I have
On the whole armor of God,
And my faith shall not be moved.
I will praise you O Lord
And I will watch my enemies be scattered.

He said, "Come." So Peter got out of the boat
And walked on the water and came to Jesus.
But when he saw the wind, he was afraid,
And beginning to sink he cried out,
"Lord, save me."
Jesus immediately reached out his hand
And took hold of him, saying to him,
"O you of little faith, why did you doubt?"
Matthew 14:29

Father, I thank you that I do not doubt in my heart.
When I doubt I am like a wave tossed to and fro.
I have faith and I will not fear because
The Lord my God is with me.

F.A.I.T.H. Confessions

Consider the lilies, how they grow:
They neither toil nor spin, yet I tell you,
Even Solomon in all his glory was
Not arrayed like one of these.
But if God so clothes the grass,
Which is alive in the field today,
And tomorrow is thrown into the oven,
How much more will he clothe you,
O you of little faith!
Luke 12:27-28

Father, I thank you that
I do not have to worry about
What I shall eat,
What I shall drink or what I shall wear.
Lord you are Jehovah-Jireh
And you are Jehovah-Shalom,
You are my provider and you are my peace.

Beloved, I pray that you may prosper
In all things and be in health,
Just as your soul prospers.
3 John 2

Father God, I thank you that it is your will that
I live in divine health and prosperity.
I am debt free and owe no man anything!
I decree it, I declare it and I receive it!

F.A.I.T.H. Confessions

And God, who knows the heart,
Bore witness to them
By giving them Holy Spirit
Just as he did to us,
And he made no distinction, between us and them
Having cleansed their hearts by faith.
Acts 15:8

Father God, I thank you that my heart is pure
And my hands are clean.
I choose to walk in faith and love
Serving others for this is the will of God.

REGINA PRICE

Trust in the Lord with all your heart,
And lean not on your own understanding;
In all your ways acknowledge Him,
And He shall direct your paths.
Proverbs 3:5-6

I will not trust in chariots or
In horses to rescue me;
I will put my trust in the name of the Lord for
The name of the Lord is my strong tower.

Be still, and know that I am God:
I will be exalted among the heathen,
I will be exalted in the earth.
Psalms 46:10

Father, I thank you that my
Faith is in the one true God
Who made heaven and earth,
He is my refuge and my strength
In Him do I put my trust.

But I have prayed for you,
That your faith should not fail;
And when you have returned to Me,
Strengthen your brethren.
Luke 22:32

Father God, my faith will forever
Remain strong because
You are praying for me and
I am praying for my brother.

F.A.I.T.H. Confessions

I have been crucified with Christ;
It is no longer I who live, but Christ lives in me;
And the life which I now live in the flesh
I live by faith in the Son of God,
Who loved me and gave Himself for me.
Galatians 2:20

I thank you that I am a friend of God and
He calls me friend! I give my life
To You O Lord in Faith so You Can
Use Me For Your Glory.

REGINA PRICE

I have fought the good fight,
I have finished the course
I have kept the faith.
2 Timothy 4:7

Father, I thank you that I am ready
To run my race with courage and faith.
I will not grow weary, and I will not faint.

F.A.T.H. Confessions

By faith the walls of Jericho
Fell down after they had
Been encircled for seven days.
Hebrews 11:30

Father, I decree and declare by faith
That the blessing of the Lord
Is on my life and no walls of lack,
Insufficiency, sickness or disease
Can come near me.

REGINA PRICE

But you, dear friends, building yourself up
On your most holy faith,
Praying in the Holy Spirit.
Jude 1:20

Father, I thank you that when I don't
Know what or how to pray, I can build up my faith
By praying in the spirit and
Trust that you will bring good out
Of every circumstance.

F.A.I.T.H. Confessions

I have chosen the way of faithfulness;
I have set my heart on your laws.
Psalms 119:30

✝

Father, I thank you that my way of faithfulness
Has helped me to hide your word in my heart
So I will not sin against you.

I can do all things through
Christ that gives me strength.
Philippians 4:13

☧

Father, I thank you that
All of my help and strength
Comes from you, my heart trusts in you and
With you all things are possible.

The Sovereign LORD is my strength;
He makes my feet like the feet of a deer,
He enables me to tread on the heights.
Habakkuk 3:19

Father, regardless of my circumstances,
My faith and my feet
Remain firm and I find
Joy in every circumstance.

ENDNOTES

http://www.wisdom-of-the-wise.com/Smith-Wigglesworth.
htm/Accessed October 2017

To order more copies

visit www.alite4life.com